D0307179

JENNY BRISTOW

cooks for the seasons
autumn and winter

JENNY BRISTOW

cooks for the seasons

autumn and winter

THE
BLACKSTAFF
PRESS

BELFAST

IN ASSOCIATION WITH UTV

contents

Autumn and winter are magical seasons that offer us the very best of ingredients. From the last rays of September sunshine through to the wintry months of January and February, and with ancient feasts and rituals a-plenty, no other time of year gives us so many opportunities to celebrate with family and friends.

Nuts and apples, pumpkins and mushrooms are all at their best in autumn. For a special harvest lunch why not make a crispy red onion tart, followed by roasted pork with a nutty apple stuffing? And for Halloween I've included recipes for some old favourites, such as steaming apple pie with little hidden parcels of coins. The broomstick pumpkin kebabs will add to the ghoulish fun!

Autumn is also the time to plan ahead and stock up for winter. My special section on preserves will tell you all about jams and chutneys and will help you to make the best of the blackberries, sloes and damsons that are in season. Remember fruit is very versatile and is also fabulous for drinks. I've included two of my seasonal favourites – elderberry cordial and sloe gin. I can guarantee they'll go down a treat!

As winter approaches, warm comforting food is just what we want. A bowl of my spiced lentil soup or a chicken and bean cassoulet should get you through those dark December days. Or try a chocolate and blackberry brownie and a *chocolat* for a perfect pick-me-up.

No book on autumn and winter would be complete without the sparkle of Christmas Day. This is a time for celebration and indulgence, so why not serve beef encrusted in juniper berries, cloves and cinnamon, followed by chilled festive cranberry cake with clementines and redcurrants? Take my word for it, this makes a very special family meal.

Using seasonal produce lets you make the most of what nature has to offer. I hope this book provides you with lots of new ideas for cooking and shows you how to make full use of the flavours, colours and aromas of autumn and winter. Enjoy!

Jenny Bristow

preserves

Preserving is all about saving the best of fruit and vegetables so that they can be enjoyed in later months. While the actual process of preserving has changed little, the greater availability of fruits, vinegars, spices and chillies has led to more exciting and imaginative combinations. The preserves in this book bring together both the traditional – after all, you can't beat a good damson jam – and the more adventurous, such as spiced chilli apple chutney.

All preserves must be placed in sterilised jars. To sterilise, wash the jars and lids well in hot soapy water and rinse thoroughly. Place them in a hot oven @ 190°C/gas mark 5 for approximately 15–20 minutes. This will kill any bacteria. Make sure you allow the jars to cool before filling.

sweet tomato pickle

makes approx 2.3kg/5lb

A tasty pickle that is ideal with cold meats and salads. This pickle is best made with fresh chillies for a truer flavour but be careful with them as they really can turn up the heat.

2.3kg/5lb tomatoes
2 dsp olive oil
2 tsp turmeric
4 tsp cumin seeds
4 cloves garlic – chopped
6 red chillies – deseeded and chopped

1 Wash and chop the tomatoes into chunks.

2 Use a pestle and mortar to crush the oil, turmeric, cumin seeds, garlic and chillies until they form a paste.

150ml/¹/4pt vegetable oil
2 inches ginger – peeled and finely chopped
225g/8oz soft brown sugar
2 tsp salt
275ml/¹/2pt white wine vinegar

3 Heat the oil in a preserving pan or a large heavy-based pan and add the ginger, sugar, salt and vinegar. Stir well until the sugar has almost dissolved, then add the chopped tomatoes and the crushed spices. Bring the mixture to the boil and cook for 25–30 mins – this will help to reduce the strength of the vinegar. Leave the pickle to cool in a covered pan, then pack into sterile airtight jars and label.

Preserves should be stored in airtight jars and, ideally, the jars should be sealed. Jam pot covers, which are readily available in supermarkets, are good for this. These contain paper discs, cellophane seals and elastic bands. After you have potted your jam or chutney, cover it at once with a disc. When the jam has cooled completely, cover with a cellophane seal and secure with an elastic band. For best results, store preserves in a cool dark cupboard.

spiced chilli apple chutney

makes approx 1.3kg/3lb

This chutney has great colour and texture and is delicious with roasted meats, breads and salads. It also contains a little oil which is a great way of developing the flavours.

900g/2lb Bramley cooking apples

1 Peel, core and dice the Bramley apples into even-sized pieces, approximately 2cm in size.

2 large onions
2 cloves garlic
1 inch ginger
2 green chillies – deseeded
1 red chilli – deseeded
4 dsp olive oil

2 Chop the onions and finely chop the garlic, ginger and chillies. Heat the oil in a large heavy-based pan. Add the onions, garlic, ginger and chillies and cook for 2–3 minutes.

2 tsp mustard seeds
1 tsp curry powder
1 tsp salt
1 tsp black peppercorns – crushed
1 tsp turmeric

3 Now add the mustard seeds, curry powder, salt, peppercorns and turmeric. Cook for 4–5 minutes to release the flavours.

350g/12oz soft brown sugar
275ml/1/2pt cider vinegar

4 Add the sugar, vinegar and diced apples. Stir slowly to ensure all the sugar dissolves. Bring the chutney to the boil. Turn down the temperature and simmer uncovered for 1 1/4–1 1/2 hrs to evaporate off the strong vinegar, until the chutney becomes thick, darkens in colour and the flavour becomes more concentrated. Pack into sterile airtight jars and label.

quick damson jam

makes approx 1.8kg/4lb

Damsons may be quite hard to come by today, but as a child we had trees and trees of them on the farm. Every autumn we'd set off loaded with baskets and come home laden with damsons. We made everything under the sun with them – we poached them and ate them with whipped cream, made pies and tarts, or else made jam. This is a very quick recipe that bottles the flavour of these tiny black plums and helps carry the memory of autumn through to the spring.

1.3kg/3lb damsons
150ml/^{1}/4pt water

1 Halve and stone the damsons. Put the stones in a muslin bag and set to one side. Place the damsons and the water in a preserving pan or a large heavy-based pan. Add the muslin bag with the stones. Simmer for 10 minutes until the fruit starts to soften. The heat in the pan will eventually force the damson stones to crack open and release pectin, which will help with the setting of the jam.

1.3kg/3lb granulated or preserving sugar

2 Reduce the temperature and allow the mixture to cool slightly. Then add the sugar and stir until dissolved. It is worth taking time to let the sugar dissolve slowly, otherwise crystallisation will occur during storage.

3 Increase the temperature and boil the jam for approximately 25 minutes or until it reaches setting point – the wrinkle test is a good way of judging this. Place a little of the hot jam on a saucer and leave it to cool slightly. Push it with your finger and if a crinkly skin forms, then the jam is at setting point. If this does not happen, continue to boil the jam and try again in about 5 to 7 minutes.

4 When the jam has set, leave it to cool slightly, then pot, seal and label.

winter essentials

cinnamon

One of the most widely used and best-loved spices, cinnamon comes from the bark of the laurel evergreen tree. Cinnamon comes in two forms – sticks and powder. The sticks are used whole or broken in half and, as they cannot be eaten, are usually removed before serving. The powder is, of course, harmless. This spice is good in cakes, biscuits, apple pies and mulled wine. It also works well in meat dishes and casseroles.

cloves

These are one of the strongest spices and should be used with care. Whole cloves resemble little nails and, because of their strong flavour and chewy texture, are not normally eaten. You can buy powdered cloves but the flavour is not as pungent. This spice is very much associated with Christmas cooking and baking. Like cinnamon, it works well in savoury and sweet dishes.

nutmeg

Although nutmeg comes in a powdered form, it is much better to use individual nutmegs. These hard nuts should be grated with a small grater to extract the flavour. Nutmeg is used widely to flavour drinks, cordials and mulled wines. It is also used in cakes and puddings. It is particularly good in Christmas cakes and fruit cakes and it also works well in cream and cheese sauces.

cardamom

This is probably one of the most underrated spices around. It is an eastern spice with a wonderful aroma and flavour and usually comes in the form of small green, brown or white pods. These have to be shelled or opened, revealing tiny black seeds which have a very strong perfume. Crush the seeds gently before adding to poached fruit, ice cream, biscuits, curries and rice dishes.

ginger

Ginger is a root vegetable – it grows underground. Its flavour is fresh and sharp and it works very well in Chinese dishes. It is very pungent and should only be used in small amounts. Peel and chop very finely or grate or crush in a garlic press. Ginger is best stored in the fridge and should keep for up to two weeks. Powdered ginger is no substitute as it has a totally different flavour.

saffron

This spice is more expensive than silver, but you only need use the tiniest amount. The reason that saffron is so expensive is that it is made from the dried stamens of the saffron crocus and it takes about 140,000 crocuses to make 1 kilogram of saffron. This spice comes in two forms – powder and, more commonly, fine threads. The threads are a fiery reddish brown, wiry looking and scrunched up. To use them in this form simply place the threads in a little hot water and leave them to infuse for a few minutes.

lentils

There are over sixty varieties of lentil, and the most popular forms are red, yellow, green or brown. Lentils are incredibly versatile and very high in fibre. They do not require soaking before use and most take only twenty

winter essentials

minutes to cook. Be careful not to overcook them as they will lose all their bite. Puy lentils are particularly good. They are a dark green colour and originate from France. Lentils cannot be stored indefinitely – after a year they will grow tougher and will be less easy to cook.

beans

Canned beans can be very good, but you just can't beat the flavour of dried beans. However, they do have a longer cooking time and most need to be soaked overnight before use. Four types of bean deserve a special mention:

butter beans – one of my favourites, soft and and fluffy in texture, mild and nutty in flavour. Mustard really brings out the best in them.

cannellini beans – very popular, often used in stews

haricot beans – these little white beans are soft in texture and are probably best known for being baked and coated in tomato sauce

kidney beans – deep red beans with a coarse texture. Follow the cooking instructions carefully as the dried beans contain natural toxins that can cause food poisoning. Kidney beans are very good in tinned form.

Pinto beans, aduki beans and black-eyed beans are not so commonly used but are also delicious and it's well worth trying them out.

oils

It's hard to beat the flavour of a good extra virgin olive oil in a dressing or as a base for a salsa. However, sunflower, grapeseed or a light olive oil are better for cooking. Whatever oil you use, my advice is to cut down on quantity; despite the benefits, there are calories in there and generous ones at that. You need only brush a pan lightly with oil when cooking and often you can get away with none at all.

chillies

Chillies are very fiery little pods that are loosely related to the pepper family. The red ones are usually milder and sweeter than the green ones. Cut the chillies in half lengthways and remove the seeds (this should reduce the heat slightly), then chop up finely. Do not touch your eyes before washing your hands as chillies can cause a burning sensation. Often, the smaller the chilli, the hotter it is. Jalapeño chillies are particularly hot. I prefer the flavour of fresh chillies although they can be bought dried. They also come in the form of powder, flakes or sauce. You can buy a variety of chilli-infused sauces such as Tabasco and harissa.

garlic

This robust member of the onion family is widely used in cooking. To prepare garlic, separate the cloves from the bulb, remove the paper and then either slice, chop or purée. I prefer the flavour of squashed or puréed garlic as it is rather sweeter than that of chopped garlic. If making a dressing, garlic is better squashed to avoid those chunky little pieces which hold their shape so well. For a change, try roasting whole cloves of garlic with the paper still on. With longer, slower cooking the garlic develops a sweeter flavour. To eat, just squeeze the garlic out of its paper.

stock

If possible, try to use fresh stock. Stock cubes work almost as well, but be careful of the higher salt content.

conversion tables

volume

1 tsp	5ml
1 dsp	10ml
1 tbsp	15ml
55ml	2floz
75ml	3floz
125ml	4floz
150ml	$1/4$pt
275ml	$1/2$pt
425ml	$3/4$pt
570ml	1pt
1 litre	$1^3/4$pt

oven temperatures

degrees centigrade	gas mark
140°	1
150°	2
170°	3
180°	4
190°	5
200°	6
220°	7
230°	8
240°	9

weights

grams	ounces
10g	$1/2$oz
25g	1oz
40g	$1^1/2$oz
50g	2oz
60g	$2^1/2$oz
75g	3oz
110g	4oz
125g	$4^1/2$oz
150g	5oz
175g	6oz
200g	7oz
225g	8oz
250g	9oz
275g	10oz
350g	12oz
400g	14oz
450g	1lb
700g	$1^1/2$lb
900g	2lb
1.3kg	3lb
1.8kg	4lb
2.3kg	5lb

measurements

millimetres	inches
3mm	$1/8$ inch
5mm	$1/4$ inch
1cm	$1/2$ inch
2cm	$3/4$ inch
2.5cm	1 inch
3cm	$1^1/4$ inches
4cm	$1^1/2$ inches
4.5cm	$1^3/4$ inches
5cm	2 inches
7.5cm	3 inches
10cm	4 inches
13cm	5 inches
15cm	6 inches
18cm	7 inches
20cm	8 inches
23cm	9 inches
25cm	10 inches
28cm	11 inches
30cm	12 inches

snacks
soups
starters

season's end tomato soup

serves 6

This is the best tasting tomato soup I've ever made. It has a deep mellow flavour with a hint of spice. It's a lovely recipe to use at summer's end when tomatoes are plentiful and at their best.

1 tsp olive oil
1 dsp red Thai curry paste
4 spring onions – finely chopped
1 inch ginger – grated
1.3kg/3lb tomatoes – diced
1 tsp caster sugar

1   Heat the olive oil in a large pot. Add the red curry paste, spring onions and ginger and cook for 2 minutes. This will allow the ginger to soften and will let the flavours develop. Next add the diced tomatoes and the caster sugar. Continue to cook for a further 7–8 minutes over a medium heat.

1 dsp fish sauce
570ml/1pt vegetable stock
275ml/¹/2pt coconut milk
450g/1lb cherry tomatoes
salt and freshly ground black pepper

2   Add the fish sauce and half of the stock and simmer for 8–10 minutes.

3   Remove the soup from the pot and blitz in a blender until you have a smooth mixture.

4   Return the soup to the pot and add the remainder of the stock, the coconut milk and the cherry tomatoes. Taste and season. Heat the soup thoroughly for a further 5–6 minutes to soften the tomatoes.

Serve with a swirl of coconut milk and slices of crusty bread.

3

warm salad of mushrooms, rocket and parmesan
with a hot mustard dressing

serves 6

This salad is great at any time of the year, but especially in October and November when mushrooms are at their best. Mushrooms are really easy to cook and are now available in many shapes and textures and come both fresh and dried.

450g/1lb assorted fresh mushrooms –
button, brown cap, oyster, chanterelle
1 dsp olive oil
25g/1oz butter
1 clove garlic – finely chopped
salt and freshly ground black pepper

1 Wash the mushrooms well and cut into assorted sizes. Leave small mushrooms whole.

2 Heat the olive oil and butter in a large pan, add the mushrooms and garlic and season with salt and pepper. You may need to cook the mushrooms in batches – if you overload the pan they will stew. Cook for 2–3 minutes – be careful not to overcook or the mushrooms will shrink.

hot mustard dressing

6 dsp olive oil
3 dsp white wine vinegar
1 tsp Dijon mustard
1 tsp of lemon juice
salt and freshly ground black pepper

Mix the oil, vinegar, mustard, lemon juice and salt and pepper together in a small bowl or in a screw top jar. Beat or shake well and leave to one side.

rocket leaves
110g/4oz parmesan shavings
2 spring onions – finely chopped

Place the rocket leaves on a large serving dish. Scatter the mushrooms on the bed of rocket leaves. Pour the mustard dressing over the salad and toss. Sprinkle with parmesan cheese and spring onions. Serve with warm crusty bread or bruschetta.

5

thai pumpkin soup

serves 8

This spicy aromatic soup is a wonderful way of using pumpkins. Serving the soup in the pumpkin shell creates a special effect and looks fabulous if you are throwing a Halloween party or having friends for dinner.

900g/2lb pumpkin flesh
1 dsp olive oil
25g/1oz butter
1 onion – finely chopped
2 inches ginger – grated
1 tsp chilli sauce or
2 red chillies – deseeded and finely chopped

1 Slice the top off the pumpkin and carefully remove all the seeds. Using a knife or a heavy spoon remove the flesh from the insides. Be careful not to cut through the shell of the pumpkin if you are using it as a serving dish, or the soup will leak out. Chop the pumpkin flesh quite coarsely.

2 Heat the oil and butter in a large heavy-based pan. When it is foaming add the onion, ginger and chillies and cook for 5–6 minutes, stirring occasionally. Next add the pumpkin flesh and stir well. Place the lid on the pan and leave to simmer for 8–10 minutes. Give the mixture a stir from time to time to prevent it sticking.

400g/14oz tin chopped tomatoes
570ml/1pt chicken stock
salt and freshly ground black pepper

3 Add the tomatoes and cook for 4–5 minutes. Now add the chicken stock and season with salt and pepper. Replace the lid and cook for a further 45 minutes.

4 Remove the soup from the heat and allow it to cool slightly. Pour the soup into a blender or liquidiser and blitz until it reaches the consistency you prefer.

570ml/1pt coconut milk

5 Return the soup to the saucepan, add the coconut milk, adjust the seasoning and cook for a further 6–7 minutes.

1 dsp of coriander or parsley – finely chopped
1 red chilli and 1 green chilli – deseeded and finely sliced

To prepare the pumpkin for use as a serving dish, ensure it is well scooped out and dry. Place in a pre-heated oven @ 180°C/gas mark 4 for 10 minutes, just to warm it through. Now add the soup. Garnish with the herbs and slices of chilli.

spiced lentil soup
with toasted cheesy bread

serves 4

Lentils come in a variety of colours, textures and flavours. They cook quickly and are very comforting and filling. This soup is packed with nourishment and flavour. I have used Puy lentils as they hold their shape better.

1 dsp olive oil
10g/¹/2oz butter
2 cloves garlic – finely chopped
1 onion – cut into large chunks
3 carrots – cut into large chunks
2 leeks – cut into rough slices
3 stalks celery – cut into rough slices

1 Heat the oil and butter in a heavy-based pan. Add the garlic and the vegetables. Place the lid on the pan and sweat the vegetables over a low heat for 10–12 minutes. Stir occasionally.

2 tsp curry powder
¹/2 tsp cayenne pepper or a dash of Tabasco sauce
2 dsp tomato paste
400g/14oz tin chopped tomatoes
salt and freshly ground black pepper
110g/4oz Puy lentils – rinsed
1.2–1.7 litres/2–3pt vegetable stock
flat leaf parsley or coriander

2 Now add the curry powder, cayenne pepper, tomato paste, chopped tomatoes and seasoning. Cook for 3–4 minutes and then add the lentils and the stock. Bring the soup to the boil and simmer for 35–40 minutes until the lentils have softened and are well cooked. Taste and adjust the seasoning if necessary.

3 Decorate with a sprig of flat leaf parsley or coriander and serve with toasted cheesy bread.

toasted cheesy bread

2 soda breads or ciabatta
1 dsp olive oil
110g/4oz mozzarella cheese – grated

1 Slice open the ciabatta or soda bread and sprinkle with oil. Toast for 2 minutes under a hot grill.

2 Sprinkle with cheese and return to the grill until the cheese melts and bubbles. Serve at once with the lentil soup.

savoury buttermilk scones

serves 8–10

This is a very simple recipe which works well for all kinds of savoury scones. This particular recipe is for Irish champ scones.

225g/8oz self-raising soda bread flour
1/2 tsp salt
25g/1oz butter
3 spring onions – finely chopped
1 egg – lightly beaten
150ml/1/4pt approx buttermilk

1 Sieve the flour and salt into a bowl.

2 Add the butter and coarsely chop through but do not rub in.

3 Add the spring onions and egg and mix well.

4 Now stir in the buttermilk to create a soft but reasonably firm dough. Shape into rounds or cut out with a pastry cutter. Bake in a hot oven @ 200°C/gas mark 6 for 12–15 minutes.

Serve with some cheese, for example Wensleydale or Stilton, and some sweet tomato pickle (see page viii).

11

pizza muffins

serves 12

This recipe is very versatile and the ingredients can be varied to suit individual tastes – try adding mushrooms, olives, peppers . . . whatever takes your fancy! Muffin trays are readily available in most department stores and supermarkets.

450g/1lb plain flour
2 tsp baking powder
25g/1oz butter – softened

1 Sieve the flour and baking powder into a large bowl. Add the butter to the flour and coarsely chop through but do not rub in.

150g/5oz roughly chopped cheese – e.g. Cheddar or Wensleydale
25g/1oz sundried tomatoes – chopped
110g/4oz bacon – diced and cooked
2 dsp parsley – chopped
salt and freshly ground black pepper

2 Add the cheese, tomatoes, bacon, parsley and seasoning and mix well.

1 dsp olive oil
425ml/³/4pt milk
2 eggs – lightly beaten

3 Mix together the olive oil and the milk and add it to the bowl along with the beaten eggs. This will form a soft doughy mixture – be careful not to over mix.

4 Divide the mixture into twelve and place in cases in a muffin tray. Each case should be about two-thirds full. Bake in the oven @ 220°C/gas mark 7 for 15–20 minutes.

Remove the tray from the oven and garnish the muffins with a little chopped parsley. Serve hot or cold.

crispy red onion tart
with salami and cashel blue cheese

serves 6–8

The base of this savoury tart can be made with a simple yeast pizza dough or with a soda bread base which I have used in this recipe. The base can be left plain or it can be flavoured with cheese or herbs.

225g/8oz self-raising soda bread flour
pinch of salt
2 dsp olive oil
1 egg – lightly beaten
125ml/4floz liquid – water, milk, or a mixture of both

1 dsp olive oil
1 red onion – cut into fine rings
350g/12oz salami
225g/8oz cherry tomatoes
225g/8oz Cashel blue cheese
fresh herbs, e.g. parsley or coriander – optional

1. Mix the flour and the salt and sieve into a bowl. Stir in the olive oil, egg and sufficient liquid to make a soft dough.

2. Turn the dough out onto a lightly floured board, knead it and shape it into a rectangle of approximately 25 x 15cm/10 x 6 inches. Place on a floured baking sheet and brush the top with a little olive oil.

3. Pour the oil into a frying pan and add the onion. Fry gently until softened. Leave the onion to cool and then sprinkle it over the top of the base. Add the salami and whole cherry tomatoes and crumble the cheese on top. Add a sprinkling of fresh herbs if you want.

4. Bake in the oven @ 200°C/gas mark 6 for 20–25 minutes until the top is crisp and golden.

Cut into slices and serve hot.

grainy mustardseed champ

serves 4

Champ is fabulous with most main courses, especially roasts and casseroles. It is also a healthy option as potatoes are low in fat. In this recipe I've added wholegrain mustard to give the champ a bit of a bite but you could also add smooth English or Dijon mustard.

8–10 potatoes – peeled and cut into chunks

150ml/^{1}/4pt low fat milk
25g/1oz butter
2 spring onions – chopped
1 dsp grainy mustard
salt and freshly ground black pepper
knob of butter

1 Cook the potatoes in boiling salted water for 20–25 minutes or until tender.

2 Gently heat the milk with the butter and spring onions for 1 minute or until bubbling.

3 Mash the potatoes. Add the milk liquid and the mustard to the potatoes and mix well. Should you prefer a creamier mash, feel free to add more milk. Season and garnish with a knob of butter.

Serve hot. For a more filling snack serve with a little bacon.

17

maple chicken wings

serves 6–8

This is ideal finger food for a party. The sweet and spicy sauce works a treat with the chicken. If you are using wooden skewers, remember to leave them in cold water for a few minutes before threading the food – this prevents them from catching fire during cooking.

barbecue and maple sauce

1 dsp olive oil
1 onion – finely chopped
50g/2oz brown sugar
1 tsp chilli paste
1 dsp soy sauce
400g/14oz tin chopped tomatoes
200ml/^{1}/3pt maple syrup

1 Heat the oil in a pan, then add the onion, sugar and chilli paste and cook for 3–4 minutes.

2 Add the soy sauce and chopped tomatoes and cook for a further 8–10 minutes until the sauce thickens slightly and concentrates in flavour.

3 Allow to cool slightly, then add the maple syrup.

chicken wings

12 chicken wings
12 rashers of bacon – optional

1 Place the chicken wings in a large dish, pour over the barbecue and maple sauce and leave to marinate for at least 15 minutes. If you want, wrap a rasher of bacon around each chicken wing before placing it in the dish. If you are wrapping the chicken in bacon, make sure that the wings are fairly small, otherwise cooking them through will be difficult.

2 Put the chicken wings on wooden or metal skewers and cook them for approximately 10 minutes either on the barbecue or on a hot grill pan. Turn often and brush with the sauce several times during cooking.

19

broomstick pumpkin kebabs
with roasted pepper relish

serves 4

These pumpkin kebabs are quick to cook and look wonderful. They're also perfect for Halloween. If you are using wooden skewers, remember to leave them in cold water for a few minutes before threading the food – this prevents them from catching fire during cooking.

roasted pepper relish

2 yellow and 2 orange peppers – halved
4 tbsp olive oil
1 tsp chilli flakes
1 dsp soft brown sugar
juice of 1/2 lemon

1 Place the peppers on a baking tray and cook in the oven @ 200°C/gas mark 6 for 10–12 minutes until softened. Alternatively, place the peppers under a hot grill until soft and slightly blackened.

2 Peel the skin from the peppers and place the flesh in a bowl with the olive oil. Blitz in a blender for 1 minute until you have a smooth paste.

3 Place the pepper mixture in a saucepan and add the chilli flakes, soft brown sugar and lemon juice. Cook for 3–4 minutes. Leave to cool.

pumpkin kebabs

225g/8oz pumpkin flesh
1 pkt large salad onions
1 yellow and 1 orange pepper – cut into 1 inch cubes
roasted pepper relish

1 Cut the pumpkin into wedges and take out the seeds. Remove the soft pumpkin flesh and cut into 1 inch chunks.

2 Steam the pumpkin over a low temperature for 7–10 minutes until slightly soft.

3 Thread alternate pieces of steamed pumpkin, salad onions and peppers onto wooden or metal skewers. Brush well with the roasted pepper relish and cook on the barbecue or under a hot grill for approximately 10 minutes or until the vegetables are tender. Turn the kebabs frequently and keep brushing them with the relish during cooking.

devilled potato skins
with a peppered chilli dip

serves 4

These crunchy spicy potato skins are great fun for a bonfire party. They're easy to eat with your fingers and are delicious on their own, dipped in soured cream or served with a peppered chilli dip.

4 large baking potatoes
110g/4oz medium Cheddar cheese – grated
1 tsp chilli-infused sunflower oil
1 pkt cooked bacon lardons
2 dsp plain yoghurt
salt and freshly ground black pepper
paprika

1   Bake the potatoes until soft and almost cooked, then cut into large wedges. Using a knife, remove the skin and set it aside. Mash the potatoes and mix in the cheese, oil, bacon and yoghurt. Season to taste.

2   Transfer the mashed potato mixture back onto each potato skin. Reheat, either on the barbecue or below a hot grill, for 2–3 minutes, until hot, bubbling and golden.

Dust with paprika and serve.

peppered chilli dip

serves 4

This dip works very well with devilled potato skins and is excellent with grilled or barbecued food.

1/2 yellow pepper
150ml/1/4pt low fat mayonnaise
1/2 red chilli – deseeded and very finely sliced
1/2 green chilli – deseeded and very finely sliced
1/2 tsp garlic – finely chopped
salt and freshly ground black pepper
sprigs of coriander or parsley

1   Roast the pepper in a hot oven or below a hot grill for 10–15 minutes until slightly blackened. Remove the skin and chop finely.

2   Place the mayonnaise in a bowl and add the pepper, chillies and garlic. Mix well and season.

Serve garnished with coriander or parsley.

rocket and red bean salad
with a sundried tomato dressing

serves 4–6

This hearty salad can be served on its own or with croutons. Feel free to vary the beans you use, but the combination of kidney beans and cannellini beans looks particularly festive.

2 slices of white or brown bread
2 dsp olive oil
400g/14oz tin kidney beans
400g/14oz tin cannellini beans
25g/1oz green olives – optional
1 dsp parsley – finely chopped
1 red onion – very finely sliced

1 tbsp olive oil
2 tbsp rice wine vinegar
2 tsp sundried tomato paste
salt and freshly ground black pepper
1/4 tsp parsley or coriander – finely chopped
1pkt rocket leaves

1 Dice the bread and spread the cubes on a baking sheet. Sprinkle with olive oil. Bake at a moderate heat for 10–15 minutes until crispy and golden. Remember to turn them occasionally.

2 Place the beans, olives, parsley and onion in a large bowl and mix well.

3 Place the olive oil, vinegar and tomato paste in a bowl and whisk. Season to taste. Add some parsley or coriander to give the dressing more colour and texture. Mix well.

4 Add the rocket leaves and sundried tomato dressing to the bean salad and toss lightly. Scatter the croutons on top and serve.

confetti salsa

serves 4–6

This dish gets its name from the attractive way the ingredients are diced and from their vivid colours.

1 small red onion
6–8 small ripe tomatoes
1/2 yellow pepper
1 dsp coriander – finely chopped
1 dsp olive oil
1 dsp rice wine vinegar
salt and freshly ground black pepper

Cut all of the vegetables into evenly shaped diced pieces and place them in a bowl. Mix well. Add the chopped coriander. Pour the olive oil and vinegar over the the salad and mix well. Season with salt and pepper.

cherry tomato, watercress and bacon clafoutis

serves 10

Clafoutis is a French dish similar to a quiche, but the main ingredients are cooked in a sauce. It's tasty, easily served, holds well and is an ideal party dish.

1 Lightly grease an ovenproof dish, either rectangular (23 x 15cm/9 x 6 inches or 23 x 20cm/9 x 8 inches) or round (25cm/10 inches in diameter). The dish should be approximately 1 1/2 inches deep as this pie will rise.

1 dsp olive oil
25g/1oz butter
450g/1lb unsmoked bacon – cut into pieces
1 onion – finely sliced
250g/9oz cherry tomatoes
225g/8oz watercress

2 Heat the olive oil and butter together in a pan. Add the chopped bacon and cook for approximately 2–3 minutes. Add the onion and cook for a further 2–3 minutes until the onion softens. Add the cherry tomatoes and watercress and heat gently for 1 minute.

4 eggs – lightly beaten
75g/3oz self-raising flour
425ml/3/4pt milk
125ml/4floz natural yoghurt or cream
110g/4oz grated cheese
1/2 tsp paprika
salt and freshly ground black pepper
parsley

3 Beat together the eggs and the flour. Add the milk gradually and beat until the mixture becomes a smooth batter. Add the yoghurt/cream and half of the cheese. Mix well.

4 Place the bacon and watercress mixture in the serving dish. Pour the sauce over the mixture and sprinkle with the remainder of the cheese and the paprika. Season and bake in the oven @ 200°C/gas mark 6 for 25 minutes until firm and golden. Garnish with parsley.

Serve hot with salad.

main courses

seared roasted white fish

with a mediterranean salsa

serves 2

Often the best way to cook fish is by the simplest of methods. This recipe uses good fresh flavoursome fish and delicious roasted vegetables.

225g/8oz baby potatoes – steamed
1 medium aubergine – sliced
4 shallots – sliced
2 plum tomatoes – chopped
1 courgette – sliced
salt and freshly ground black pepper

1 Place all the vegetables on a grill pan or in a roasting tin. Season with salt and pepper. Leave to one side.

2–3 dsp olive oil
juice of 1 lemon
a few basil leaves – torn
2–3 dsp balsamic vinegar

2 Mix together the olive oil, lemon juice, basil and balsamic vinegar. Pour the mixture over the vegetables and place them under a hot grill for 8–10 minutes or put them in the oven @ 200°C/gas mark 6 for 12–15 minutes.

25g/1oz caster sugar
1 inch ginger – finely chopped
juice and zest of 1 lime
2 fillets of fish, e.g. cod or haddock

3 Mix the sugar, ginger, juice and zest to form a marinade.

4 Place the fish in a dish and cover with the marinade. Leave for 10 minutes. Cook on a grill pan for 3–4 minutes on each side.

5 Remove the fish from the pan and serve with the mediterranean salsa.

roasted autumn pork

with a nutty apple stuffing

serves 4

The secret in cooking pork is to seal in the flavour before roasting. This recipe for roasted autumn pork makes a wonderful dish and will ensure your crackling is done to perfection. The nutty apple stuffing works a treat with the pork, but is entirely optional.

1.5–1.8kg/3¹/4–4lb loin of pork – boned
sea salt
1 dsp olive oil

Dry the outside of the pork thoroughly with some kitchen roll. This will ensure that the crackling becomes really crisp. Score the rind of the pork with a sharp knife and rub it with sea salt. Heat the oil in a large pan or dish. Place the pork, rind down, onto the hot pan for 1–2 minutes. This will help it to crisp up. Transfer the pork to a roasting tin, pour over a little oil and sprinkle with salt. Cook in the oven @ 190°C/gas mark 5 for 30 minutes per 450g/1lb, plus an extra 30 minutes, or until cooked.

nutty apple stuffing

25g/1oz butter
1 dsp olive oil
1 onion – finely chopped
1 cooking apple – finely diced
50g/2oz roasted hazelnuts – finely chopped
1 tsp thyme – chopped
150g/5oz white breadcrumbs
1 egg – beaten
salt and freshly ground black pepper

1 Heat the butter and oil in a pan. Add the onion and cook until it is softened. Add the apple, hazelnuts and thyme. Mix well but do not overcook. Add the breadcrumbs and egg. Season with salt and pepper and mix until the stuffing binds.

2 Pack the stuffing into the centre of the meat. Tie the pork securely with a string to keep the stuffing intact. Sear the pork and roast in the oven in the way described above.

To make this a really special dish, roast some apples, plums, figs and red onions alongside the stuffed pork.

33

lemon mustard potatoes

serves 6

Two excellent ideas for potatoes. These dishes are served hot and work well with with any kind of roasted meats.

900g/2lb baby potatoes

1 Wash and halve the potatoes and either boil or steam until tender. Cooking time will depend on the size of the potatoes.

zest of 1/2 lemon
1tsp wholegrain mustard
125ml/4floz natural yoghurt
salt and freshly ground black pepper
chives or parsley – finely chopped

2 Drain the potatoes and place in a bowl. Add the lemon zest, mustard and yoghurt immediately, while the potatoes are still warm. Season with salt and pepper. Mix well and serve garnished with chives or parsley.

baked red potato salad

serves 6

900g/2lb red potatoes
1 lemon
4 dsp crème fraîche
2 dsp parsley – finely chopped
salt and freshly ground black pepper

1 Prick the potatoes all over and place them on a baking sheet with the lemon. Cook in the oven @ 200°C/gas mark 6. The potatoes will need at least 1 hour but the lemon may be removed after 20 minutes – the heat should have softened and sweetened it. Don't worry if it blackens during cooking. Squeeze the juice from the lemon and mix it with the crème fraîche and parsley. Season.

2 When 1 hour has elapsed, remove the potatoes from the oven and cut them into wedges. Leave to the side to cool.

When the potatoes have cooled, pour the dressing over them, toss and serve.

firecracking sausage and onion casserole

serves 8–10

This is an ideal supper or party dish that is a little bit different. The crispy apple slices, golden onions and bitter-sweet sauce are a real treat.

25g/1oz butter
1 tsp olive oil
4 cloves garlic
2 red onions – cut into wedges
1 onion – cut into wedges
1 inch ginger – finely chopped

1 Melt the butter in a large casserole dish and add the oil. Heat through. Add the garlic, onions and ginger. Cook until crispy.

900g/2lbs sausages
4 red apples – sliced
4 green apples – sliced
1 tbsp soft brown sugar

2 Fry the sausages until they are golden and crisp, using just a hint of oil. Add the apple slices and let them cook in the juice of the sausages until they too become golden and crispy. Sprinkle the sugar over the apples and the sausages and cook for a further minute.

310ml/11floz unsweetened apple juice
1 dsp chilli sauce
salt and freshly ground black pepper
400g/14oz tin cannellini beans – optional

3 Place the sausages and apples in the casserole dish. Pour in the apple juice and the chilli sauce and mix well.

4 Season with salt and pepper and, if adding beans, do so at this stage. Place in the oven @ 200°C/gas mark 6 for 35–40 minutes.

Serve hot with rice, pasta or potatoes.

37

chicken and bean cassoulet

serves 6–8

Very tasty bean stew which can be made with chicken, beef, lamb or pork. The type of bean used in this dish can also be varied, but usually white beans work best. Try cannellini beans for a change.

1 dsp olive oil
10g/¹/2oz butter
6–8 chicken joints (skin on) –
thighs or drumsticks

1 Heat the oil and butter in a large ovenproof dish. Add the chicken pieces, skin side down, and cook for 2–3 minutes until the skin starts to brown. Turn and cook on the fleshy side for another 2–3 minutes.

2 onions – cut into rings
2 carrots – cut into chunks
2 parsnips – cut into chunks
2 leeks – roughly sliced

2 Add the onion rings, carrots, parsnips and leeks to the dish and replace the lid. Cook for 6–7 minutes to allow the flavours to develop.

225g/8oz haricot beans – tinned
(dried beans will need
to be soaked)
2 tomatoes – cut into chunks
1 dsp tomato paste
4 dsp cider vinegar
1 dsp caster sugar
150ml/¹/4pt apple juice
570ml/1pt chicken stock

3 Add the beans, chopped tomatoes and tomato paste to the dish.

4 Mix the vinegar, sugar, apple juice and stock. Add this to the dish and mix well.

900g/2lb potatoes –
cut into 1cm/¹/2 inch thick slices
1 egg – lightly beaten
salt and freshly ground black pepper

5 Top the casserole with a layer of overlapping potatoes. Brush with the beaten egg. Season with salt and pepper and bake in the oven @ 170°C/gas mark 3 for 1¹/2 hours. This dish is cooked slowly to allow all the flavours to develop.

winter vegetable stirfry with griddled duck breast

serves 2

There is such a wide variety of duck breasts now available. These breasts can be cooked and served whole or cut into slices. Either way, the flavour and moistness of the duck is excellent.

4 spring onions – chopped
2 chillies – deseeded and finely chopped
1 inch ginger – finely chopped or grated
2 cloves garlic – finely chopped
1 red pepper – cut into slices
200g/7oz mangetout
200g/7oz assorted mushrooms, e.g. button, chestnut or shitake – chopped
4 stalks bok choi
2 x 110g/4oz duck breasts
salt and freshly ground black pepper
1 dsp sesame oil
1 dsp olive oil
2 dsp soy sauce
4 dsp plum sauce

1   Prepare the vegetables and leave to one side.

2   Trim the duck breasts and score the skin. Be careful not to cut through the fat. The scoring will allow the skin to crisp up during cooking. If you're watching your fat content, simply remove the skin.

3   Just before cooking, sprinkle the duck with salt and pepper and place on a hot grill pan, skin side down. Cook for 3–4 minutes, draining off the fat as it comes out of the meat. Turn the duck and cook for a further 3–4 minutes. Total cooking time can average between 8–12 minutes, depending on how pink you like your duck.

4   While the duck is cooking you can prepare the stirfry. Place the sesame and olive oil in a good sized wok and heat. Add the spring onions, chillies, ginger and garlic. Cook for about 2 minutes, then add the pepper, mangetout, mushrooms and bok choi. Cook for a further 2–3 minutes. Be careful not to overcook the vegetables – you want them to have a bit of bite. Add the soy sauce and plum sauce and toss the vegetables around. Serve at once.

Remove the duck breast from the pan. Slice if you wish and serve with the sizzling vegetables.

41

lightly smoked fish lasagne
with pine nuts, celery and spinach

serves 8

A dish made with undyed smoked fish and a delicious sauce. If you find the flavour of the Stilton cheese a little strong, you can replace it with a milder cheese, such as Cheddar, mozzarella or, one of my favourites, cambozola. This dish is ideal for entertaining as it holds well.

450g/1lb undyed smoked fish, e.g. cod
or haddock
4 dsp milk
25g/1oz butter

1   Place the smoked fish on a plate, spoon over the milk and dab with butter. Cover and cook in the microwave or poach gently for 3–4 minutes until the fish is soft enough to flake into fairly coarse pieces. Remove any bones.

sauce

25g/1oz butter
25g/1oz flour
275ml/¹/2pt milk
1 egg yolk
200ml crème fraîche
110g/4oz Stilton – crumbled

2   Melt the butter in a pan. Add the flour and milk and mix until you have a smooth liquid. Bring the mixture to the boil. Reduce the temperature and add the egg yolk, crème fraîche and the Stilton.

225g/8oz 'no cook' lasagne
450g/1lb spinach – washed and dried
2 stalks celery –
cut into wafer-thin pieces
50g/2oz pine nuts

3   To assemble the lasagne, place a layer of lasagne in a rectangular dish. Top with fish, spinach, celery and half of the sauce. Place another layer of lasagne on top and cover with the remainder of the sauce. Scatter the pine nuts over the top of the lasagne and bake in the oven @ 200°C/gas mark 6 for 25–30 minutes, or until cooked and golden brown.

43

medieval saffron stew

serves 6–8

An ideal dish when you want to prepare in advance.
A combination of fruit and either lamb or pork can be used
for this dish. The fruit can be fresh or dried. The hint of
cinnamon brings out the best in the flavours.

1 dsp saffron threads
2 dsp water

1 Place the saffron threads in a bowl with the water and leave
   to infuse for 10 minutes until the water is yellow.

1 dsp olive oil
900g/2lb pork or lamb pieces

2 Heat the oil in a pan and add the meat. Cook over a high
   heat for 6–7 minutes until the meat has browned. You may
   need to cook the meat in batches – if you overload the pan
   the meat will stew instead of browning.

225g/8oz baby onions
1 tsp garlic – finely chopped
1/2 tsp paprika

3 Add the baby onions, garlic and paprika and cook for
   2–3 minutes.

1/2 tsp cinnamon
110–225g/4–8oz apricots, depending
on taste
400g/14oz tin chopped tomatoes
1.2 litres/2pt stock (vegetable or
chicken)

4 Add the cinnamon, saffron threads and liquid, apricots,
   tomatoes and stock. Turn the heat down and leave to simmer
   for 1–1 1/4 hours with the lid on. If you do not want to keep
   this dish on the hob, it can be cooked in the oven @
   190°C/gas mark 5.

50g/2oz whole almonds
50g/2oz pistachio nuts

5 Add the nuts to the casserole dish approximately 15 minutes
   before serving.

Serve with basmati rice or toasted bread.

45

hot grilled prawns with mushroom mozzarella

serves 4

You can use frozen prawns for this dish, but it is even better if you can buy them fresh and juicy from your fishmonger or from the fish counter in your supermarket.

350g/12oz large shelled prawns – defrosted if necessary
juice of 1 lemon
salt and freshly ground black pepper

1 Sprinkle the prawns with a little lemon juice, salt and pepper.

200g/7oz pasta shells
1 dsp olive oil
2 leeks – finely sliced
200g/7oz mushrooms – sliced
200g/7oz Parma ham or Serrano ham
1/2 tsp paprika
275ml/1/2pt single cream
110g/4oz mozzarella cheese – grated

2 Heat a large pan of boiling water. Add a little salt and cook the pasta according to the instructions on the packet. When it is cooked, drain, return to the pan and leave to one side.

3 Heat the oil in a large pan. Add the leeks and mushrooms and cook gently for 2–3 minutes.

4 Add the ham, prawns, paprika and cooked pasta. Mix well. Pour the cream into the mixture and stir well. Do not overcook or you may require more liquid.

5 Transfer the mixture to a lightly greased ovenproof dish. Sprinkle with mozzarella cheese and place in a hot oven @ 200°C/gas mark 6 for 6–7 minutes, or below a hot grill for 4–5 minutes until bubbling and golden.

Serve with bread and salad.

christmas day

lettuce soup

serves 6–8

This is a delicately flavoured soup, light in texture, and ideal as a starter for your Christmas meal.

3 cos lettuce

1 Wash the lettuce and remove the outside leaves. Tear the remaining leaves into pieces.

25g/1oz butter
1 tsp olive oil
2 potatoes – peeled and diced
6 spring onions – finely chopped

2 Heat the butter and oil in a pan, add the potatoes and the spring onions and cook gently for 4–5 minutes. Do not allow the mixture to brown.

3 Add the chopped lettuce and cook with the lid off until it begins to wilt.

2.3 litres/4pt chicken stock
salt and freshly ground black pepper

4 Add the stock and seasoning and let the mixture simmer for 15 minutes, again with lid off as this helps to preserve the colour of the soup. Be careful not to overcook the soup as this will also spoil the colour.

1 tsp lemon juice
1 dsp soured cream
pinch of freshly grated nutmeg

5 Blitz the soup in a blender until smooth and return it to the pan. Adjust the seasoning if necessary. Add the lemon juice and mix through.

Serve with a swirl of soured cream and sprinkle lightly with freshly grated nutmeg. Delicious with crusty bread or Melba toast.

spiced crusted beef
with braised ruby red onions and shallots

serves 8–10

Sides of beef have been popular at Christmas since Elizabethan times. Choose a good-sized joint of beef – this will ensure that you have some left over to serve cold with salads and chutney the next day.

25g/1oz juniper berries – crushed
3–4 cinnamon sticks – finely crushed
2–3 dsp peppercorns – finely crushed
2–3 sprigs rosemary – stalks removed
3.2kg/7lb joint of beef –
sirloin, fillet or fore rib
1 dsp olive oil
25g/1oz butter
275ml/^{1}/2pt red wine or port
275ml/^{1}/2pt stock

1 Prepare the crust by mixing together the berries, cinnamon, peppercorns and rosemary. Wipe the beef dry with some kitchen roll and brush with a little olive oil. Roll the beef in the crushed spices until it is well covered. Heat the oil and butter in a large heavy-based frying pan. Brown the meat over a medium heat for 3–4 minutes.

2 Remove the meat from the heat and place in a well-oiled roasting dish. Cook in the oven @ 200°C/gas mark 6. Allow 12 minutes, 15 minutes or 20 minutes per 450g/1lb, depending on whether you like your meat rare, medium or well done. After 15 minutes cooking, add the wine and stock to the roasting dish. Baste the meat regularly during cooking. When cooked, use the juices in the base of the pan to make a gravy. Serve with braised ruby red onions and shallots.

braised ruby red onions and shallots

8–10 small red onions – peeled and
halved, depending on size
250g/9oz shallots – peeled

1 Blanch the onions and shallots by placing them in a large pot of boiling water for 2 minutes. Drain.

25g/1oz butter
25g/1oz soft brown sugar

2 Melt the butter in a frying pan. Add the sugar, onions and shallots and cook over a high heat until lightly browned.

1 dsp redcurrant jelly
150ml/^{1}/4pt port
salt and freshly ground black pepper

3 Add the redcurrant jelly, port and seasoning and leave to cook for 6–7 minutes, stirring occasionally, until the onions are soft and the liquid has reduced and thickened.

53

vegetable christmas casserole

serves 6

This casserole is made with the best of the season – parsnips, onions and potatoes. It is also a dish made with Christmas in mind and combines the flavours of Stilton cheese and chopped pistachio nuts or hazelnuts.

1 onion – sliced
900g/2lb parsnips – sliced thickly
2 potatoes – sliced
1 small aubergine – sliced
1 beef tomato – sliced
2 dsp olive oil
25g/1oz butter

1 First, prepare all the vegetables.

2 Heat the oil and butter in a pan. Add the onion and fry for 2–3 minutes. Now add the parsnips and cook for a further 3–4 minutes.

1 tsp nutmeg
salt and freshly ground black pepper

3 Grease a deep 20cm/8 inch round tin and place half of the parsnips and onions inside. Next add a layer of potato, a layer of aubergine, a layer of tomato and top with the rest of the parsnips and onions. Sprinkle with a little nutmeg and season with salt and pepper.

275ml/¹/2pt cream
110g/4oz brown breadcrumbs
110g/4oz Stilton
110g/4oz chopped nuts –
pistachio or hazelnut

4 Pour the cream over the vegetables and top with the brown breadcrumbs. Crumble the Stilton cheese over the vegetables and breadcrumbs.

5 Cook the casserole in the oven @ 180°C/gas mark 4 for 30–35 minutes until the vegetables are cooked and the topping is bubbling and golden brown. Add the chopped nuts approximately 15 minutes before serving.

55

chilled festive cranberry cake

serves 8–10

Cranberries are readily available throughout the winter and are particularly popular around the festive period. This pudding is very light and is a delicious alternative to some heavier desserts.

175g/6oz biscuits, e.g. digestive, almond or hazelnut
75g/3oz butter
1 dsp honey
1/2 tsp cinnamon

1 Place the biscuits in a bag and crush into fine crumbs with a rolling pin. Alternatively, blitz them in a food processor.

2 Melt the butter in a saucepan and add the honey and cinnamon. Add the crushed biscuits and mix well. Line the base of a round springform tin (20–23cm/8–9 inches) with greaseproof paper and butter the sides well. Transfer the mixture to the tin, pressing down well and leave to cool.

450g/1lb cream cheese, e.g. Philadelphia or mascarpone
50g/2oz caster sugar
zest of 1 lemon
zest of 1/2 orange
4 drops vanilla essence
150ml/1/4 pt whipping cream
150ml/1/4 pt Greek yoghurt
25g/1oz caster sugar

3 Place the cream cheese, caster sugar, zest and vanilla essence in a bowl or in a food processor and mix until smooth.

4 Pour the mixture onto your biscuit base and level it out. Place the tin in the fridge for approximately 1 hour.

5 Whip the cream firmly and mix with the yoghurt and caster sugar.

6 Remove the tin from the fridge and spoon the cream mixture onto the cake. Return the tin to the fridge and allow to chill for a further 30 minutes.

200g/7oz cranberries
25g/1oz caster sugar
zest and juice of 1 orange
1 dsp arrowroot or cornflour
1 dsp cold water
mint leaves to decorate

7 Place the cranberries, sugar, orange zest and juice in a saucepan. Bring to the boil and continue to heat gently until the cranberries begin to pop. This should take about 4–5 minutes. Do not overcook the fruit or its appearance will be spoiled.

8 Mix the arrowroot with the cold water. Add to the saucepan and heat for 1 minute. Leave the mixture to cool.

9 Remove the tin from the fridge and, just before serving, pour the cooled cranberries onto the cheesecake. Decorate with a few mint leaves and serve.

sweet mincemeat lasagne
with a cointreau cream sauce

serves 8

This sweet mincemeat lasagne is made with filo pastry and topped with a simple Cointreau sauce. Filo pastry is convenient and makes a light alternative to mince pies which can be very high in fat. The tangy Cointreau sauce complements the mincemeat perfectly.

1 egg white – lightly beaten
1 dsp olive oil
8–10 sheets filo pastry – defrosted

1   Mix the egg white and the olive oil and brush each separate layer of pastry lightly. This should stop it becoming soggy during cooking.

225g/8oz sweet mincemeat

2   Place the mincemeat in a bowl and mix gently to soften. This will help to spread it evenly over the filo pastry.

1 egg – beaten

3   Use 4 sheets of the filo pastry to layer the bottom of a rectangular tin. Spread the mincemeat evenly over the top of the pastry. Place 4 more sheets of the pastry over the mincemeat, crumpling the pastry around the edges. Brush the top with the beaten egg.

25g/1oz caster sugar
1/2 tsp cinnamon

4   Mix the caster sugar and cinnamon and dust the top of the lasagne. Bake in the oven @ 200°C/gas mark 6 for 15–20 minutes or until cooked and golden brown. Filo pastry can burn quite easily, so watch it carefully during cooking.

cointreau cream sauce

275ml/1/2pt whipping cream
2–3 dsp Cointreau
zest of 1/2 orange
zest of 1/2 lemon

Beat the cream until it is quite thick. Fold in the Cointreau and the orange and lemon zest.

Remove the lasagne from the oven and serve it hot or cold with the Cointreau cream sauce.

59

desserts

lemon yoghurt cake

with poached blackberries in an irish mist

serves 8

This tangy pudding is made with melted white chocolate to give it a smooth creamy texture. The lightly poached blackberries complement the lemon flavour perfectly and a hint of Irish Mist liqueur gives the dish an extra twist but is entirely optional.

110g/4oz almond biscuits
25g/1oz butter
2 dsp honey

1 Blitz the biscuits in a food processor or use a rolling pin to crush. Melt the butter in a pan over a low heat and add the honey. Warm through for 30 seconds. Now add the biscuits and mix well. Continue to heat for a further 1–2 minutes. Line a 23cm/9 inch springform tin with greaseproof paper and butter the sides. Transfer the mixture to the tin, and press down well.

400g/14oz good quality white chocolate
4 egg yolks
25g/1oz icing sugar
zest of 3 lemons
570ml/1pt Greek yoghurt
(or 1/2 single cream and 1/2 yoghurt)

2 Melt the chocolate in a bowl over a pan of hot water. Put to one side to cool. Beat the eggs and sugar in a separate bowl over a pan of warm water. Now add the lemon zest, the cooled chocolate and the yoghurt to the egg yolks and sugar and mix well. The mixture may thicken but don't panic – keep mixing and it will eventually become smooth. Pour the whole mixture over the biscuit base and leave to set in the fridge for 1–2 hours.

poached blackberries

1 tbsp water
25g/1oz sugar
225g/8oz blackberries
1 dsp bramble jelly
2 dsp Irish Mist – optional
sprig of mint

Heat the water in a saucepan and add the sugar. Stir well until the sugar has dissolved. Next, in with the blackberries and poach gently for 2 minutes until the fruit has softened but still retains its shape. Now add the bramble jelly and the Irish Mist. Leave to cool.

Place the cooled lemon yoghurt cake on a plate. Serve with the poached blackberries and a sprig of mint.

hazelnut meringue
with elderberry syllabub and poached plums

serves 8–10

This nutty meringue is dark and crunchy and works a treat with the plums and the elderberry syllabub. It can be made as a large dessert or piped as individual meringue nests. The recipe for the cordial can be found on page 93.

4 egg whites
200g/7oz caster sugar
25g/1oz soft brown sugar
110g/4oz toasted hazelnuts – finely chopped

1　Whisk the egg whites in a bowl until they form firm peaks. Add half of the caster sugar and continue to beat for a further minute. Next fold in the rest of the caster sugar, the soft brown sugar and the nuts. Do not overbeat – you need to keep as much air in the mixture as possible.

2　Line a baking sheet with greaseproof paper. Use a 23cm/9 inch plate to trace an outline. Transfer the mixture to the baking sheet, flatten out and, with a palette knife, form into the shape of the circle. Cook in the oven @ 150°C/gas mark 2 for 20 minutes. Then reduce the temperature to 140°C/gas mark 1 for approximately 30–40 minutes.

3　Take the meringue out of the oven and leave to cool before gently removing the greaseproof paper from the bottom.

poached plums

225g/8oz plums – stoned
25g/1oz demerara sugar
1 dsp water

Place the plums, sugar and water in a saucepan. Heat gently for 2–3 minutes until the plums soften. Remove from the pan and leave to cool.

elderberry syllabub

juice of $^1/2$ lemon
50g/2oz caster or icing sugar
275ml/$^1/2$pt double cream
2 dsp elderberry cordial

Place the lemon juice and sugar in a large chilled bowl and whisk together. Add the cream and continue beating until the mixture thickens slightly. Finally add the elderberry cordial and mix thoroughly.

To serve, pour the syllabub over the meringue and top with the poached plums.

traditional apple pie

serves 8

I have so many different recipes and ideas for apple pies, tarts and crumbles. This apple pie is one of the simplest to make but it has all the essentials – a good crumbly shortcake pastry and lots of Bramley apples. I've also suggested that you hide coins in the cake – this makes it ideal for Halloween and other festive occasions.

250g/9oz plain flour
50g/2oz ground almonds
175g/6oz butter – softened
zest of 1/2 lemon
1 egg yolk
1 dsp cold water

6 Bramley apples – peeled, cored and finely sliced
50g/2oz caster sugar
juice of 1 lemon
8–10 cloves
coins
milk or beaten egg

1　For ease this pastry can be prepared in a blender. Place the flour, almonds, butter, zest, egg and water in the blender and blitz until the mixture just binds.

2　Remove the pastry from the blender, wrap in clingfilm and place in the fridge for 15 minutes.

3　Place the apples in a dish and sprinkle with sugar, lemon juice and cloves. Leave to sit for 10 minutes.

4　Wrap some individual coins securely in a little greaseproof paper.

5　Remove the pastry from the fridge and divide it in two. Roll out each piece so that it will fit a deep 23cm/9 inch ovenproof plate. Place one piece of the rolled out pastry on the plate and spread the apples, sugar and cloves evenly on top. Arrange the wrapped coins on top of the apples.

6　Brush the edge of the pastry with cold water before laying the second piece of pastry on top. Squeeze the edges of the pastry together to seal them. Make a slit on the top of the pie to let the air through. Brush with a little milk or beaten egg and bake in the oven @ 200°C/gas mark 6 for 20–25 minutes until golden.

Dust with icing sugar and serve warm with cream or yoghurt.

pear and brazil nut tart

serves 8

Pears are a very undervalued fruit and in this tart they are combined with a tasty sponge, Brazil nuts and a crumbly topping.

25g/1oz flour
25g/1oz brown sugar
25g/1oz butter – softened
1 tbsp Brazil nuts – coarsely chopped

1   Sieve the flour into a bowl and mix in the sugar. Add the butter and rub in until the mixture becomes crumbly. Mix in the Brazil nuts. Leave to one side.

110g/4oz butter – softened
110g/4oz caster sugar
3 eggs – lightly beaten
175g/6oz self-raising flour
1/2 tsp baking powder
1–2 dsp natural yoghurt

2   Cream together the butter and sugar for thirty seconds, then add the eggs, flour, baking powder and yoghurt. You should have quite a soft mixture.

3   Line the bottom of a 23cm/9 inch tin with greaseproof paper.

2 large ripe pears

4   Peel, core and slice the pears.

4 dsp Greek yoghurt or soured cream

5   Pour the cake mixture into the tin. Arrange the slices of pear on top and pour over the Brazil nut topping. Bake in the oven @ 190°C/gas mark 5 for 45 minutes or until the cake is firm to the touch.

Serve with Greek yoghurt or soured cream.

pears poached in saffron syrup

serves 4

Saffron is a very delicate spice with a wonderful yellow colour. It gives fruit a unique flavour and is delicious not just with pears, but also with apples and plums.

10–15 threads of saffron
2 dsp warm water
275ml/½pt water
50g/2oz granulated sugar
4–6 ripe pears
ice cream or natural yoghurt

1 Prepare the saffron by placing the threads in a bowl with the warm water. Leave to infuse for 8–10 minutes.

2 Place the saffron threads and liquid, water and sugar in a saucepan and bring to the boil to dissolve the sugar.

3 Peel and core the pears.

4 Add the pears to the saucepan and poach very gently over a low heat until they show signs of softening. Remove the pan from the heat and allow to cool.

Present the pears fanned with the syrup and a little ice cream or natural yoghurt. The pears can be served warm or cold.

warm winter fruit
on french fruit toast with cinnamon ice cream

serves 4   This can be used as a dessert but is also good as a quick snack.

2 eggs – lightly beaten
125ml/4floz milk
25g/1oz butter
1 dsp sunflower oil
4 slices of fruit loaf

1   Lightly beat the eggs and milk in a bowl. Heat the butter and oil in a frying pan. Soak the slices of fruit loaf in the egg mixture for 30 seconds and fry gently for 1 minute on either side. Dry on a little kitchen paper to absorb any excess oil.

125/4oz dried apricots
4 clementines – peeled and sliced
2 pears – peeled, cored and sliced
125ml/4floz water
25g/1oz granulated sugar
1 cinnamon stick

2   Mix all the fruit in a bowl and leave to one side. Heat the water, sugar and cinnamon stick in a saucepan for 2–3 minutes. Add the fruit to this mixture and poach gently for 2 minutes. Do not allow the fruit to break down. Remove the cinnamon stick (this may be kept for decoration).

225g/8oz vanilla ice cream
25g/1oz dark soft brown sugar
1/2 tsp cinnamon

3   Place scoops of ice cream in an ovenproof dish. Sprinkle with the brown sugar and cinnamon and place under a very hot grill until the the top is bubbling, golden and crunchy.

Place the fruit loaf on a plate and serve with the fruit and the ice cream.

73

chocolate mousse cake
with cranberries, clementines and redcurrants

serves 8

I have a passion for chocolate cake and this one has a very interesting texture. It can be served on its own, but cranberries and clementines give it a really festive look.

110g/4oz good quality plain chocolate
3 eggs – separated
25g/1oz plain flour
1/2 tsp baking powder
110g/4oz butter
50g/2oz ground almonds
110g/4oz caster sugar

1   Grease a round 20cm/8 inch tin and line the base with greaseproof paper. Leave to one side.

2   Break the chocolate into pieces and melt in a large bowl over a pan of hot water. In a separate bowl, beat together the egg yolks until smooth. Mix the flour and baking powder and sieve.

3   Add the butter and then the egg yolks to the chocolate and mix well. Next add the flour and baking powder, the ground almonds and 3/4 of the caster sugar and mix.

4   In a separate bowl, beat the egg whites and the remainder of the sugar until the mixture becomes white and fluffy. Add the egg whites to the chocolate mixture and fold in carefully until everything is well mixed. Transfer to the lined tin and bake in the oven @ 180°C/gas mark 4 for 40–45 minutes.

4 clementines
25g/1oz soft brown sugar
2 dsp water
25g/1oz caster sugar
110g/4oz fresh cranberries
sprigs of mint
redcurrants

5   Carefully remove the pith and peel from the clementines and cut them into assorted shapes. Reserve any juice that may come out of them. Place them on a baking tray, dust with brown sugar and place them under a hot grill until they blacken slightly. Leave to one side to cool.

6   Place the water and caster sugar in a saucepan. Add the cranberries and the reserved juice from the clementines. Poach the cranberries until they show signs of softening and popping. Leave them to cool, then mix them with the clementines. Spoon them over the chocolate mousse cake just before serving. Decorate with mint leaves and a few redcurrants.

roasted fruit

with a hot cinnamon sauce

serves 6–8

This is a hot fruit salad with a difference. The cinnamon sauce gives it a suitably festive feel.

2 pears – peeled, cored and sliced
2 plums – stoned and cut into segments
1 peach – stoned and cut into segments
110g/4oz whole cherries – stoned
110g/4oz raspberries
110g/4oz strawberries
4 clementines – peeled and sliced
liqueur – optional
zest and juice of 1/2 lemon – optional
25g/1oz caster or icing sugar

1 Place all the fruit in an ovenproof dish. If you like, drizzle a little liqueur, such as Irish Mist or Cointreau, over the fruit. Alternatively you can use a little lemon juice. Sprinkle with the sugar. Brown the fruit below a hot grill for 2–3 minutes. You can also use a blow torch.

4 egg yolks
4 dsp caster sugar
1/2 tbsp orange juice
1/2 tsp cinnamon

2 Place the egg yolks and sugar in a bowl and whisk together until the mixture is light and fluffy. Now place the bowl over a large pan of simmering water. Continue to beat the mixture for about 10 minutes, either by hand or with an electric mixer, until it becomes creamy, light and frothy – it will lose its eggy flavour as it cooks. Add the orange juice and cinnamon and cook for a further minute, beating continuously.

25g/1oz icing sugar
25g/1oz demerara sugar
50g/2oz flaked almonds
redcurrants
sprigs of mint

3 Pour the sauce over the fruit and sprinkle with a mixture of icing sugar, demerara sugar and flaked almonds. Place the fruit below the hot grill for another 2–3 minutes until the top is brown and bubbling.

Serve the fruit decorated with redcurrants and sprigs of mint.

frosted berries with toasted hazelnuts
with nutty cardamom biscuits

serves 2

This is a simple idea for a dessert. You can vary the fruit with the season, but the blackberries do go very well with these biscuits.

225g/8oz blackberries
25g/1oz sugar
1 dsp water
1 dsp liqueur, e.g. Cointreau
or Kirsch – optional
110g/4oz Greek yoghurt
50g/2oz hazelnuts
225g/8oz vanilla or mascarpone
ice cream
mint leaves

1 Place the blackberries, sugar and water in a saucepan. Bring to the boil and simmer gently for 2–3 minutes. Allow to cool and add the liqueur. Fold half of the berry mixture into the yoghurt.

2 Toast the hazelnuts below a hot grill until they are golden and brown. Chop finely.

3 Serve this dessert in tall glasses. Place some berries in the glass, followed by a layer of ice cream and finally add the yoghurt and berry mixture. Decorate with chopped hazelnuts and a sprig of mint. Serve with nutty cardamom biscuits.

nutty cardamom biscuits

110g/4oz hazelnuts
175g/6oz butter or margarine
25g/1oz icing sugar
75g/3oz caster sugar
6–8 cardamom pods
225g/8oz plain flour
a few drops of vanilla essence
icing sugar for dusting

1 Toast the hazelnuts below a hot grill until they are golden and brown. Chop finely.

2 Place the butter, icing sugar and caster sugar in a large bowl. Stir well until the the mixture becomes white and creamy. Shell the cardamom pods and discard. Crush the seeds and add them along with the nuts to the bowl. Sieve in the flour and continue stirring. Add a few drops of vanilla essence. Stir again.

3 Turn the dough out onto a floured surface and knead gently to remove any cracks and to bind the dough. Wrap the dough in clingfilm and place in the fridge for 15 minutes.

4 Remove the dough from the fridge and roll it into a cylinder shape. Cut into rounds approximately 1.5cm thick. Place on a baking sheet and cook in the oven @ 180°C/gas mark 4 for 15–20 minutes.

Remove from the oven and leave to cool. Dust with icing sugar.

tray bakes
and
treats

chocolate and blackberry brownies

serves 12

A quick idea that uses one of my favourite combinations –
blackberries and chocolate. Raspberries also work well in this
dish. Use white or dark chocolate – either way these brownies
are delicious.

3 eggs
175g/6oz caster sugar
110g/4oz good quality white or dark
chocolate
75g/3oz butter or margarine –
softened
110g/4oz self-raising flour for cakes
110g/4oz fresh blackberries
50g/2oz chocolate chips – optional
cocoa powder or icing sugar
for dusting

1   Beat together the eggs and half of the sugar until you have a
    light creamy mixture. Using a spatula, fold in the remainder
    of the sugar. Do not over beat the mixture at this stage.

2   Break the chocolate into pieces and melt in a bowl over a
    pan of warm water. Add the butter to the chocolate and stir
    until both have completely melted.

3   Add the melted chocolate to the egg mixture and mix. Fold
    in the flour and the blackberries.

4   A few chocolate chips can added at this stage to give more
    texture to the brownies.

5   Transfer the brownie mixture to a lined square 15cm/6 inch
    tin and bake in the oven @ 180°C/gas mark 4 for 25–30
    minutes.

When cooked and firm, remove from the oven and cool on
a tray. Cut into squares and dust with cocoa powder or icing
sugar.

shortbread biscuits

Shortbread is probably one of the most popular biscuits I know – crumbly and comforting with a wonderful buttery taste.

225g/8oz plain four
50g/2oz cornflour
75g/3oz caster sugar
225g/8oz butter
icing sugar for dusting

1   Place the dry ingredients in a bowl. Cut the butter into the mixture and rub in. Initially this will make a crumbly mixture, but will eventually come together as a single piece of dough.

2   Flour a board or a worktop and turn the dough out. Knead gently and then roll out.

3   You have three options at this point:

> use a cutter to make the biscuits
>
> roll the dough into a log shape and cut into rounds approximately 1.5cm thick
>
> place the dough in a round 18cm/7 inch tin and pack down well

4   Whatever you decide, prick the dough with a fork and bake in the oven @ 180°C/gas mark 4 until the shortbread takes on a very light golden colour. Cooking time will depend on the size of shortbread you decide to make and will take anything from 10 to 20 minutes.

When the shortbread is cooked and is still warm, dust with icing sugar.

For a variation on traditional shortbread, try adding caraway seeds, dried blueberries, pine nuts or almonds. Simply add 25g/1oz of your chosen ingredient to the dry ingredients at stage one.

toffee apples

serves 6–8

Toffee apples are just the ticket for Halloween. You can use red or green apples but make sure they are quite small.

6–8 small red or green apples
225g/8oz sugar
2–3 tbsp cold water
pinch of cream of tartar
wooden ice lolly sticks

1 Wash and dry the apples and put them to one side.

2 To make the toffee, place the sugar in a small saucepan and add the water. Put the pan over a low heat and stir the mixture until the sugar has completely dissolved. Now add the cream of tartar – this helps to prevent the sugar from crystallising – and bring the mixture to the boil. Turn the temperature down and simmer gently for approximately 10 minutes until the liquid turns golden brown.

3 Remove the pan from the heat and allow the bubbles to subside. Quickly dip the apples into the toffee and leave them to cool on greaseproof paper or on a kitchen surface that has been rubbed with a little oil.

Children – a word of warning. Please do not be tempted to make these toffee apples without an adult as the toffee is very hot and can be dangerous.

mixed berry muffins

serves 12

Muffins have become so popular because they are tasty, versatile and very easy to make. This recipe makes a very tasty snack for any time of the day and can be prepared in advance.

275g/10oz self-raising cake flour
2 tsp baking powder
1 tsp cinnamon
1 tsp mixed spice
110g/4oz mixed dried berries, e.g. cranberries or blueberries
50g/2oz nuts, e.g. walnuts or Brazil nuts

1 Place all the dry ingredients – the flour, baking powder, cinnamon, mixed spice, dried berries and nuts – into a large bowl and mix well.

2 eggs – lightly beaten
110g/4oz butter – softened
275ml/¹/2pt milk

2 Add the eggs, butter and milk to the bowl and mix lightly (no longer than 1 minute). Be careful not to over mix.

3 Transfer the mixture to cases that have been placed in a muffin tray – the mixture should make 12 large or 24 small muffins. Bake in the oven @ 190°C/gas mark 5 for 15–20 minutes.

Christmas idea

This recipe can be easily adapted and presented as a Christmas gift. Simply take all of the dry ingredients, place them in a sealed airtight jar and label.

drinks

sloe gin

Sloes are the fruit of the blackthorn tree and are in season between August and October. Sloe gin was traditionally used as a medicine or for a nightcap. It can be used as a flavouring for poached fruit or in cream toppings. It's also delicious on its own.

450g/1lb sloes
175g/6oz granulated sugar
275ml/¹/2pt gin

1 Sterilise the bottle in whch the sloe gin is to be stored by rinsing well with boiling water.

2 Wash and dry the sloes and prick them with a fork.

3 Place the sloes and the sugar in alternate layers in the bottles. Top with enough gin to cover the sloes.

4 Seal and label the bottles and store in a cool dark cupboard for at least 2–3 months. During this time the sugar will dissolve and the gin will turn a dark rosy pink. During the first week shake the bottle every day or so and at least once a week during the next 2–3 months. This will help the sugar to dissolve and will bring out the juice from the sloes.

5 Strain off the liquid, discard the sloes and store the gin in a clean sterilised bottle.

elderberry cordial

900g/2lb elderberries
275ml/¹/2pt water
225g/8oz caster sugar

1 Wash the berries and remove their stalks. Now place the water and the berries in an ovenproof container with a lid. Heat in the oven @ 110°C/gas mark 1/4 for 2–3 hours.

2 Strain the juice through a fine sieve and pour it into a large pan. Add 225g/8oz sugar for every pint of juice. Simmer for 20–25 minutes.

3 Pour into sterile bottles and store in the refrigerator. The cordial will keep for up to 3–4 weeks.

hot apple cider

2 oranges – sliced
juice of 2 oranges
juice of 2 lemons
2 cinnamon sticks
50g/2oz granulated sugar
2.3 litres/4pt apple juice
2 green apples, 2 red apples – sliced
10 cloves
1/4 tsp ginger

1   Place the sliced oranges, orange juice, lemon juice, cinnamon sticks, sugar and apple juice in a large pan. Heat gently to dissolve the sugar and then simmer for 10–15 minutes.

2   Stud the sliced apples with cloves and place on a baking sheet. Bake in the oven @ 180°C/gas mark 4 for 5–10 minutes. Be careful not to overcook – you just want to soften the apples.

3   Add the ginger to the mulled apple cider and heat for a further 5 minutes.

4   Remove the orange slices and add the baked apples with cloves. Heat through for a further 2 minutes and serve. The cinnamon stick should be removed before serving but can be used for decoration.

The addition of the baked apples is optional.

spiced ginger beer

1 orange
1 lemon
12 cloves
2 bottles good ginger beer –
2.3 litres/2pt approx
1 inch ginger – grated
2–3 cinnamon sticks

1   Cut the orange and lemon in half and stud them with the cloves. Place on a baking sheet and bake in the oven @ 180°C/gas mark 4 for 15–20 minutes to sweeten and intensify the flavours.

2   Place the ginger beer in a large saucepan and add the studded oranges and lemons, ginger and cinnamon sticks. Bring to the boil. Turn the temperature down and simmer gently for 6–7 minutes to allow the flavours to infuse.

3   Remove from the heat and allow to cool slightly before serving in warmed glasses. Serve with a slice of orange.

mulled wine

No drink reminds me of cold winter nights and celebrating the festive season like mulled wine. It has a fabulously rich burgundy colour and a wonderfully spicy aroma. This is a great drink to serve at parties and is a warming welcome for friends and unexpected guests. Because this drink is flavoured and spiced, you don't need to use expensive wine.

3 oranges – unpeeled
10–12 cloves
1.7 litres/3pt water
2–3 cinnamon sticks
225g/8oz granulated sugar
2 bottles red wine
1 apple and 1 orange to serve

1 Roughly cut up the oranges and place them in a saucepan with all the other ingredients, except the red wine.

2 Heat the mixture gently until the sugar has dissolved and then bring to the boil. Simmer for 30 minutes, then strain. If you do not want to make the mulled wine immediately, refrigerate this mixture until required. This will keep for approximately two weeks.

3 To complete the mulled wine, return the mixture to the pan, bring to the boil and add the wine. Heat through. Do not boil as this will spoil the colour.

4 Slice the apples and oranges and stud them with cloves for decoration. Place them in the pan. Heat for a further 2 minutes and serve.

A great variation on this is mulled cranberry juice – simply replace the red wine with cranberry juice.

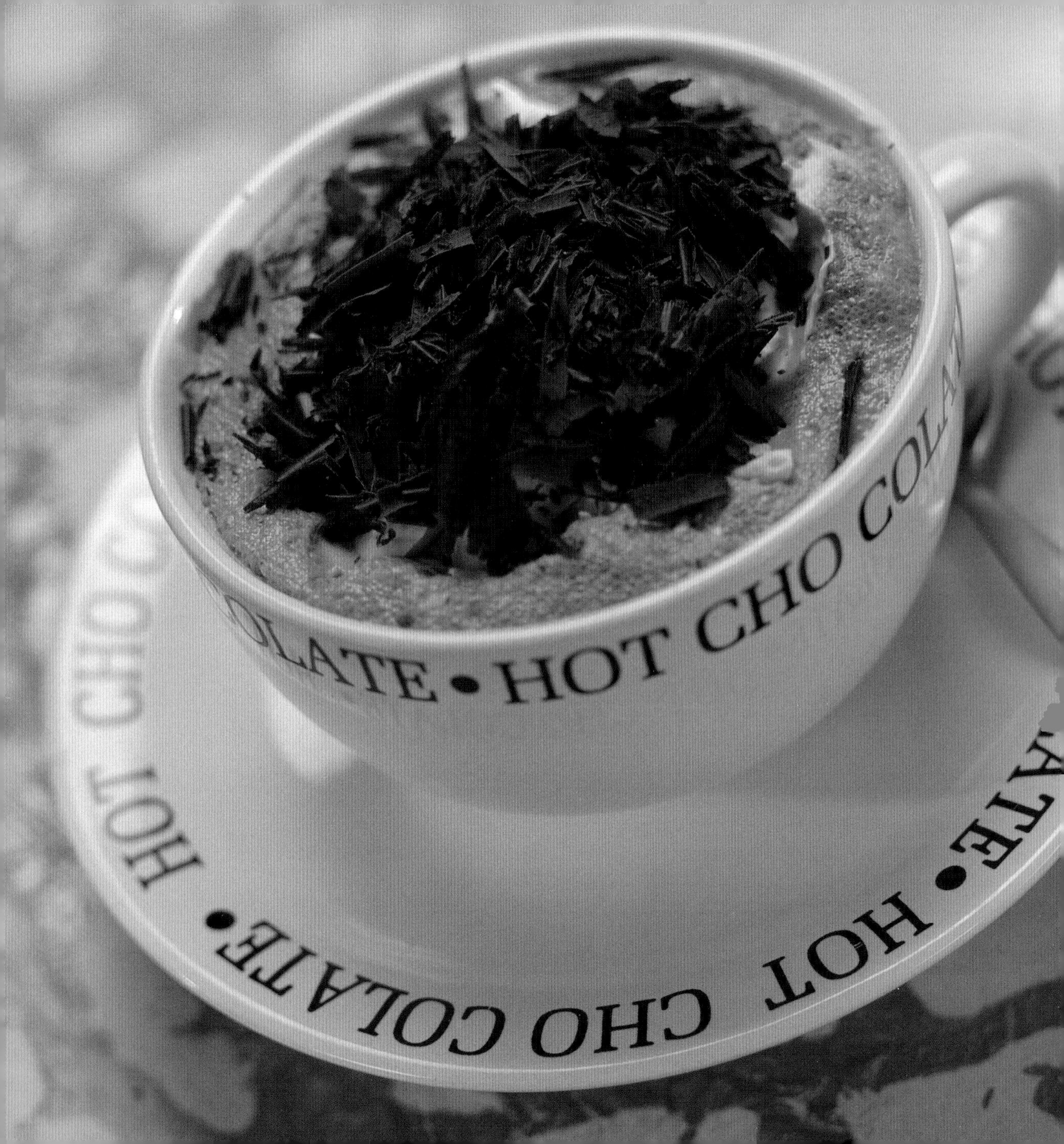
LATE • HOT CHO COLA
HOT CHO COLATE • HOT

chocolat

There is something warm and comforting about this drink. It reminds me of childhood and is a great pick-me-up on a cold winter's day.

1 tsp chocolate powder
1 tsp honey
1 dsp hot water
275ml/^{1}/2pt milk
1 dsp lightly whipped cream
25g/1oz good quality dark chocolate – grated
pinch of nutmeg or cinnamon

1   Mix the chocolate powder, honey and water.

2   Warm the milk in a pan and when it is almost bubbling, add the chocolate mix and stir well.

3   Pour the mixture into a large cup or mug and top with whipped cream. Sprinkle with chocolate and a little nutmeg or cinnamon.

iced coffee

Iced drinks are becoming increasingly popular and this recipe works well with coffee or chocolate. Vary the amount of coffee or chocolate you use depending on your own taste.

150ml/^{1}/4pt water
1 tsp coffee
1 tsp caster sugar
1 scoop vanilla ice cream
1 scoop chocolate ice cream
275ml/^{1}/2pt chilled milk
25g/1oz good quality dark chocolate – grated

1   Heat the water in a pot. When it is hot, add the coffee and mix well. Add the sugar and stir until it has dissolved. Leave the mixture to cool.

2   Place the scoops of ice cream in tall glasses. Pour the coffee mixture over the top, followed by the milk. Decorate with the grated chocolate and serve with a long spoon.

acknowledgements

It has taken the mind-blowing efficiency of everyone at Blackstaff Press to help produce a book of this quality. My thanks go to Anne Tannahill, Wendy Dunbar, Patsy Horton and Bairbre Ryan – you are all such a joy to work with. Special thanks also go to photographer Robert McKeag and to food stylist Colette Coughlan.

   In the production of both the book and the television series, I have been lucky enough to work with many people whom I consider the best in the business. So thanks to Bernie Morrison, producer and director, for her professionalism and her sense of fun; to the crew – Sam Christie, P.J. McGirr,

Billy Rowan, Mary McCleeve, Ronnie Martin and Ivan Heaslip – for their hard work and imaginative contributions; to Alan Bremner at UTV who continues to commission the programme and allows us to grow and experiment; to Orla McKibbin, also of UTV, for her vision and support; to Maureen Best, Vera McCready and Nan Millar for all their work behind the scenes; to Donna McAleese and Geri McAfee, hair stylists at Peter Mark; and to Mark Bell and Ian Gowdy who edited the programme.

Thanks are also due to Helen Turkington at the Fabric Library, Cookstown and Newbridge, County Kildare; to Paddy McNeill of Beeswax, Kilrea, for sourcing the free-standing dressers and cupboards; to Sally at Floral Designs, Ballymena, for the flower arrangements; to Nicholas Mosse Potter, Enniskillen; Michelle Kershaw and Diane at Lakeland Plastics; Maud Hamill at Calor Gas; Laura Ashley, Belfast; to Hilary and Ian Robinson at Presence, Newtownards, for so much hard work in coordinating china, pottery and dishes for the programmes; to Helen Bedford at Le Creuset; Jim Patton at Red Fyre Cookers, Belfast; Millcraft Handmade Kitchens, Sydenham Road, Belfast; Sydney Stevenson Agencies, Bangor, and Meyer Prestige; and to all the many family and friends who contributed to the programme and helped to make it such an enjoyable experience.

index

First published in 2002 by
The Blackstaff Press Limited,
Wildflower Way, Apollo Road,
Belfast BT12 6TA,
in association with UTV

© Jenny Bristow, 2002
© Photographs, McKeag & Co, 2002
All rights reserved

Jenny Bristow has asserted her right under the
Copyright, Designs and Patents Act 1988
to be identified as the author of this work.

Printed in Northern Ireland by W & G Baird Limited
A CIP catalogue record for this book
is available from the British Library

ISBN 0-86540-724-0

www.blackstaffpress.com

Jenny chats with Bernie
Morrison, producer of
UTV's *Jenny Bristow Cooks for
the Seasons*